High Loan-to-Value Mortgage Lending

High Loan-to-Value Mortgage Lending

Problem or Cure?

Charles W. Calomiris
and Joseph R. Mason

The AEI Press

Publisher for the American Enterprise Institute
WASHINGTON, D.C.
1999

Available in the United States from the AEI Press, c/o Publisher Resources Inc., 1224 Heil Quaker Blvd., P.O. Box 7001, La Vergne, TN 37086-7001. To order, call toll free 1-800-269-6267. Distributed outside the United States by arrangement with Eurospan, 3 Henrietta Street, London WC2E 8LU England.

ISBN 0-8447-7125-2

1 3 5 7 9 10 8 6 4 2

THE AEI PRESS
Publisher for the American Enterprise Institute
1150 17th Street, N.W., Washington, D.C. 20036

Printed in the United States of America

Contents

Foreword

America's financial markets are in many respects the wonder of the world for their efficiency and dynamism. But they are also constrained by numerous obsolete regulatory policies, and their very dynamism makes them a tempting target for new political impositions. The U.S. government is awash in proposals to revise financial market regulation—in some cases to remove or streamline long-standing regulatory policies, in others to add new government controls. The stakes for the U.S. economy are considerable.

This pamphlet is one of a series of American Enterprise Institute studies of a broad range of current policy issues affecting financial markets, including regulation of the structure and prices of financial services firms; the appropriate role of government in providing a "safety net" for financial institutions and their customers; regulation of securities, mutual funds, insurance, and other financial instruments; corporate disclosure and corporate governance; and issues engendered by the growth of electronic commerce and the globalization of financial markets.

The AEI studies present important original research on trends in financial institutions and markets and objective assessments of legislative and regulatory proposals.

Prepared by leading economists and other financial experts, and distributed to a wide audience of policy makers, financial executives, academics, and journalists, these studies aim to make the developing policy debates more informed, more empirical, and—we hope—more productive.

CHRISTOPHER DEMUTH
President
American Enterprise Institute

1
Introduction

High loan-to-value (HLTV) mortgage lending is an innovative, fast-growing means of consumer finance. Despite its appeal to borrowers and lenders, some observers fear that such lending may produce undesirable fragility among consumers and lenders or within the economy as a whole. Only after systematically examining the service niche of this industry, its management practices and lending policies, the changing nature of the consumer finance marketplace, and the role of consumer lending in the economy can one judge whether HLTV lending is a beneficial innovation or whether the public interest would be served by trying to limit such lending. The current study is our effort to make such a systematic examination.

Chapter 2 provides an overview of the development of the HLTV industry and its consequences for consumer finance. Chapter 3 focuses on the demand side of the market—the characteristics of HLTV borrowers and the underlying motives that lead consumers to prefer HLTV loans to other forms of consumer lending. Chapter 4 provides a similar perspective on the supply side of the market—the particular means of financing the demand for HLTV lending, especially the growth of securitizations. Chapter 5 analyzes the risks from HLTV lending. Chapter 6 applies the results of chapters 2–5 to the current policy debates surrounding HLTV lending, particularly the proposed imposition of *cram-down* on HLTV lenders. Chapter 7 presents the conclusions and recommendations of the study as a whole.

Today's HLTV lending evolved from Title I lending. Growth in demand during the 1980s reflected the appeal of HLTV loans for liquidity-starved consumers in the wake of corporate downsizing and real-estate market declines. Recent growth in HLTV lending largely reflects its advantages for consumers and bankers alike compared with credit card lending, for which it is a close substitute. The advantage to lenders is the reduced probability of default because of linking debt to the borrower's home. Consumer debt collateralized by the borrower's home is effectively a senior claim on his income, backed by an asset that would otherwise be protected from seizure by creditors if he were to file for bankruptcy.

Because linking consumer credit to a home mortgage can impose nonpecuniary (for example, foreclosure) costs on defaulting borrowers, it strongly deters defaulting. In essence, HLTV lending provides consumers a means of committing to prevent avoiding debt repayment by filing for bankruptcy under the current permissive bankruptcy laws. Consumers benefit from reduced default risk in the form of lower interest rates.

Chapter 3 describes the high average quality of HLTV loans. We clarify the distinction between HLTV loans (which are sometimes incorrectly equated with subprime loans) and true subprime lending. Although both are mass-marketed (because of the high attrition during the origination phase), HLTV loans are typically granted only to sound credit risks (A or A-minus borrowers). HLTV loans have been referred to as subprime only because their high loan-to-value (LTV) ratio does not conform to the traditional guidelines of the major secondary mortgage market underwriters, the Federal National Mortgage Association (Fannie Mae) and the Federal Home Loan Mortgage Corporation (Freddie Mac). This is quite different from lending to properly defined (economically) subprime borrowers who are substandard credit risks. The industry recognizes this distinction and now refers to loans that do not satisfy traditional mortgage guidelines as *nonconforming*, reserving the term *subprime* only for loans with substandard credit risk.

Chapter 5 discusses the risks entailed in HLTV lending and shows that such lending does not magnify aggregate risk to consumers, bankers, or the economy. Indeed, the ability to tie consumer debt to the consumer's home reduces the probability of default. Consumers are less likely to choose high debt levels when default would place their homes at risk. Thus, the movement from other consumer credit (like credit card debt) into HLTV debt likely reduces both leverage and default risk. Furthermore, the lower interest rates on HLTV loans make default less likely.

Not only do HLTV borrowers and lenders gain from reduced default risk, but the economy as a whole is more stable as the result of HLTV lending. Enhanced consumer liquidity and reduced consumer default risk stabilize aggregate demand. Moreover, because HLTV lending can rely on securitization for the bulk of its financing (see chapter 4), it provides a more diversified, and thus a more stable, source of consumer credit.

HLTV lending involves special risks, which chapter 5 analyzes. One conceivable special risk results from the unique financing technology of HLTV lending, that is, the possibility of an interruption in the supply of capital through private secondary mortgage markets. But the possibility of a significant interruption is remote. Multiple safeguards are built into the structure of securitized debt to protect debtholders and thus to limit their incentive to flee in response to heightened risk. Experienced investors are sophisticated enough to understand how to measure and to manage the risks of HLTV loans. The fundamental characteristics of both HLTV (and even subprime) lending are now well understood, as evidenced by the recent entrance of Fannie Mae and Freddie Mac into these arenas.

Chapter 5 also discusses other HLTV lending risks such as the alleged results from consumer *reloading* (using credit cards to increase debt after an HLTV debt consolidation loan) and *churning* (using lower debt-to-income ratios from an undisclosed HLTV debt consolidation loan to obtain another, larger HLTV loan). The chapter points out that, to the extent that these phenomena occur, they would also happen in the absence of HLTV lending. In fact, HLTV debt provides safeguards that may be superior to other forms of consumer credit in preventing such practices.

Although some critics view HLTV lending as an unsound or even reckless activity that magnifies consumer lending risk, our review of the evidence leads us to conclude just the opposite. HLTV lending is a clear improvement in financial technology that reduces the costs of consumer credit while promoting the stability of the financial system. New regulations like the proposed cram-down limit on HLTV lending would undermine the unique advantages of HLTV lending. Such limits would be harmful to the interests of consumers and to the economy as a whole.

2
The Evolution of HLTV Lending

Origins

In recent years a number of home equity lenders have expanded their product lines by offering new products with borrowing limits up to 125 percent of the ratio of the loan amount to the value of the underlying property. The introduction of such products departs significantly from traditional mortgage underwriting principles, which held that the underlying LTV ratio was the primary indicator of credit quality. Underwriting principles for the new, high loan-to-value lending are adopted from the consumer lending sector and combine a borrower's LTV with credit scores intended to predict capacity and willingness to repay. These typically are based on characteristics such as the borrower's income, wealth, and occupation.

As HLTV lending has become an accepted product in the mortgage industry, hundreds of finance companies, credit unions, savings and loans, traditional banks, and even conservative mortgage banks have begun offering HLTV mortgages. Currently only a few firms dominate such lending. These include FirstPlus Financial, the Money Store, Empire Funding, and Master Financial. These dominant players are finance companies, but as the industry grows, it is attracting other financial intermediaries. Gordon Monsen, former managing director, PaineWebber, estimated that as of September 1997 forty mortgage banks had begun originating HLTV loans (Talley 1997). Since Fannie Mae and Freddie Mac recently began accepting these A to A-minus–rated loans for securitization, more traditional mortgage lenders are expected to enter the field. (A-rated borrowers are considered prime candidates for loans. See chapter 3 for a brief explanation of loan-rating classifications.)

Recent industry history reveals that HLTV loan products evolved from such predecessors as the Title I loans that home equity lenders have been underwriting since the 1930s, home improvement loans, second-lien debt-consolidation programs, and new approaches to combining debt consolidation and cashout (unsecured) lending (Fitch IBCA 1998b, 2).

Many HLTV specialists, including FirstPlus Financial, "began in the Federal Housing Administration (FHA) Title I or other home improvement loan program and moved primarily into debt consolidation and cashout 125 LTV mortgages" (Fitch IBCA 1998b, 2). FHA Title I loans are originated under the National Housing Act of 1934. These loans are used for specific purposes allowed under that act, such as home improvement. Although the loan proceeds are dedicated to a specific set of home improvements and there is a maximum size to the loan, there has never been any LTV limit. Therefore, these lenders have been making HLTV loans for some time now.

But HLTV lending and Title I lending are not identical. Title I lenders underwrite loans in the context of a government program where the credit quality is insured for up to 90 percent of the loan amount (although insurance coverage on each originator's pool is limited to 10 percent of the pool). Furthermore, the pool of borrowers may not be entirely comparable: since the government program exists to provide credit to a broader range of borrowers than would otherwise obtain it, Title 1 borrowers have, on average, lower credit quality than HLTV borrowers. Nevertheless, the principles of HLTV lending and Title I lending are essentially the same.

Making Title I loans has a disadvantage compared with HLTV loans: Title I lending involves much red tape. As lenders learned how to underwrite such loans effectively, they saw advantages to underwriting home improvement loans outside the Title I program and used the home as collateral even when there was little home equity as the result of a high LTV ratio. These home equity loans carried the added advantage for consumers of a tax deduction on the interest. Over time, home equity lending of this sort became commonplace for many traditional mortgage lenders. Eventually home equity lending became "a logical extension of a savings institution's traditional role of serving the needs of the American family in meeting its housing-related expenses. In addition, home equity lending is proving profitable for institutions seeking to diversify beyond traditional first mortgage lending" (Wilson 1997, 22).

During the 1980s, when tax law changes did away with write-offs of nonmortgage loan interest, home equity loans became attractive to even more consumers—as well as important as a new product line for lenders looking for a competitive edge. As more consumers began to substitute home equity loans for other types of consumer loans, financial institutions began seeking ways to make the application process easier. For many lenders the transformation of consumer debt into home equity debt became routine. Michael Richardson, vice president of lending at the Mid-Atlantic Federal Credit Union in Maryland, describes how his institution uses "the equity in the home as the second collateral for the loan. If a person wants to purchase a car, that serves as the primary collateral. Then, if the [borrower] wants to write off the interest, the [lender] puts a second lien on the home" (Courter 1998, 29). The mortgage is one—but not the only or even the most important—source of protection that creditors seek when making HLTV loans.

The recession of the early 1990s coincided with the transformation of this brand of home equity–consumer lending into the distinct HLTV mortgage market niche of today. Three major factors related to the recession contributed to this development. First, the population of borrowers with impaired credit increased substantially, particularly in regions with the highest unemployment and highest property value declines. Consumer debt of marginally impaired borrowers, particularly those with high credit card debt, increased demand for debt consolidation loans. Second, lenders with stagnant loan volumes sought new business lines to stay competitive. Third, and perhaps most important, secondary mortgage markets matured during this era. The growth of secondary mortgage markets reflected multiple influences, including new technological capabilities, the volume of failed bank assets securitized by the Federal Deposit Insurance Corporation and the Resolution Trust Corporation, and the strong demand for high-yield investments among foreign investors. Those influences deepened U.S. capital markets significantly, ameliorated the U.S. recession, and expanded the domestic loan market.

These three factors combined to create new opportunities for both high-risk (subprime) and low-risk consumer borrowers, made possible by HLTV lending. An account of the importance of HLTV lending for borrowers with a subprime credit profile is provided in Faulkner & Gray's *Home Equity Lending Directory*:

> The recession of 1990–1992 and the end of the Cold War did more for [subprime] lending than any other events in history. . . . Thanks to corporate downsizing and the shrinkage of the defense industry (which employed millions of U.S. workers) many consumers saw

their credit ruined when layoffs translated into late bill payments and bankruptcies. . . . This was tough on the consumer, but it did create a lending opportunity. . . . Subprime lenders with origination networks in California, New England, and parts of the Sunbelt have done well because they are now lending money to these workers.

But the growing attraction of HLTV lending was not limited to the subprime category of borrowers. The 1990s have seen rising rates of consumer default and bankruptcy among borrowers. For higher-quality consumer borrowers, the main attraction of HLTV lending is an interest rate substantially lower than that typically available on credit cards. For lenders, the main attraction of such lending is the reduced incentive for borrowers to default.

Recently bankruptcies have been widespread, even for borrowers who can repay their debts but choose to take advantage of lenient bankruptcy laws. Because some or all housing wealth and wages are exempt from creditor recourse, many prosperous consumers file for bankruptcy even though they could easily pay their outstanding debts. Michelle White (forthcoming) estimates that roughly one-quarter of American households could profit from filing for bankruptcy under Chapter 7, and roughly half that number have been willing to take advantage of the legal (but typically unwarranted) discharge of debt.

The key advantage of HLTV lending compared with nonmortgage consumer lending is the reduced probability of voluntary default that comes from tying a debt to the consumer's home. Consumer mortgage debt (1) is collateralized by an asset (and is thus a senior claim on consumer income); (2) is a claim on an asset that would otherwise be protected from seizure by creditors if borrowers file for bankruptcy; and (3) is a form of debt that can impose nonpecuniary (for example, foreclosure) costs on defaulting borrowers. Linking consumer credit to a home mortgage not only reduces losses to creditors when defaults occur, it also discourages consumers from defaulting because it places lenders in a stronger bargaining position. The nonpecuniary costs to consumers of a mortgage default can be large, including the loss of their home through foreclosure. Even if the lender chooses not to foreclose, his holding a lien on the mortgaged property limits the consumer's options to sell or to improve the home. At the same time the borrower typically benefits from the reduced incentives to default under HLTV lending through interest rates that are significantly lower than under, for example, credit card lending.

The attraction of HLTV lending in limiting the risk of voluntary default became increasingly apparent during the 1990s. Consumers who would have been willing to default on their nonmortgage debt did not walk away from their mortgage debts, even when economic conditions deteriorated. Bankers came to understand that *willingness to pay* was as important as *capacity to pay* when gauging consumer default risk and that mortgage debt enjoyed lower risk because of mortgagors' greater willingness to pay. Low-risk consumer borrowers were attracted to HLTV lending because the increasingly competitive market for lending allowed them to capture the lion's share of the gains from their credible commitment to reducing their default risk.

Today's HLTV Industry and Beyond

Americans now use the equity in their homes to finance their children's college education, to consolidate credit card or other debts, to make home improvements, or to purchase new cars. For the consumer a home equity loan is an attractive option, mostly because a large part of the interest paid on such loans—up to the fair market value of the dwelling—is tax deductible. Home equity loans are also far cheaper than credit card debt and may be paid over longer terms than most other borrowing alternatives.

HLTV lenders extend home equity loans for the same purposes and with the same advantages as home equity lenders but do so by offering second liens with a combined total LTV of more than 100 percent. HLTV lenders making these loans have largely turned away from traditional mortgage lending standards in favor of underwriting standards similar to those used for unsecured (primarily, credit card) loan products.

Because there is little mortgage collateral to seize in the case of default, HLTV lenders, like unsecured lenders, focus on other measures of creditworthiness. In many cases high leverage relative to the mortgaged property does not translate into high loan risk. "A survey released by the Consumer Bankers Association in June 1997 painted a sanguine picture of home equity lenders routinely making high-LTV loans to borrowers who are older, richer, and more creditworthy than before" (Prakash 1997, 16). HLTV loans tend to be made to upper-middle-class borrowers who may be overextended but who would not risk their prime credit profile with bankruptcy or default (Timmons 1997k). "The classic [HLTV] customer . . . is a homeowner with significant equity in a home and a high level of debt on credit cards who is looking to consolidate" (White and Levanthal 1997, 50).

One of the key attractions for consumers of HLTV loans is the interest savings. Average interest rates charged on securitized loans originated by the biggest four HLTV lenders during 1997 ranged from 13.75 percent to 13.97 percent (Fitch IBCA 1998b). RAM Research's CardTrak survey—designed to help consumers identify the *lowest* interest-rate credit cards and therefore a downward-biased measure of credit card interest rates as a whole—quotes a range of interest rates for low-interest, zero-fee gold cards from 13 percent to 19 percent for April 1998.

Consumers seeking to borrow large amounts using credit cards face average interest rates significantly higher than those on HLTV loans, and industry analysts clearly link the growth in HLTV lending to the interest savings enjoyed by consumers. According to "Better Prepays on High LTV Mortgages Expected in 1998," *Inside B&C Lending,* March 2, 1998, one analyst forecasts a "migration of the lowest risk borrowers away from the credit card market into high LTV mortgages as consumers take advantage of an arbitrage opportunity that could be worth 500 basis points."

While consumer gains from lower interest rates on HLTV loans are undoubtedly substantial, the 500 basis points of interest savings cited above probably exaggerates consumer savings. Borrowers typically pay points on HLTV loans in addition to interest. By charging points, HLTV lenders can reduce the interest rate on their loans, which limits the prepayment risk from market declines in interest rates (see the discussion of prepayment risk in chapter 4). According to unpublished reports, points paid on HLTV loans average roughly 7 percent of the value of the loan. Assuming (conservatively) a six-year maturity for the HLTV loan, the annual cost of points would be roughly 120 basis points.

The substantial cost savings from HLTV borrowing can significantly improve a consumer's debt-to-income ratio—and reduce the probability of bankruptcy. "The typical borrower at the time of origination has about 45 percent debt [to income] ratio, which is about the maximum. . . . After debt consolidation in the high LTV loan the ratio drops to around 37 percent," Jeff Moore, president of Mego Mortgage of Atlanta, claimed (Muolo 1997, 73).

The deductibility of interest payments on the portion of HLTV loans up to 100 percent of the property value magnifies their advantages for consumers relative to credit card debt. A consumer borrowing up to 100 percent through a second-trust loan, for example, and facing a 19 percent annual (pretax and after-tax) credit card interest rate, a 15 percent pretax financing cost (annual interest and points) on second-trust borrowing, and a 50 percent marginal tax rate would reduce the pretax borrowing cost by 400 basis points—but would reduce his after-tax borrowing cost by 1,250 basis points.

A number of indicators point to substantial growth potential for HLTV lending. Industry experts estimate that consumers hold approximately $4 trillion in home equity (Wilson 1997, 27). Given the potential for mortgaging that equity, Peter Rubenstein, head of credit research at PaineWebber, believes the HLTV market is likely to double to $15 billion during 1998 and soon could "skim the cream off the $500 billion credit card industry" (Clark 1998, 38).

Reflecting the shift in consumer borrowing toward secured borrowing, asset-backed security (ABS) issuance—which measures activity in the secondary market for financing these mortgages—of home equity loans has finally surpassed credit cards, which have traditionally been the largest sector of the ABS market outside conforming mortgages sold by Fannie Mae and Freddie Mac (Flanagan, DiSerio, and Asato 1998, 46). "Home equity loan ABS issuance now commands a 34-percent share of the ABS market, up from only a 12-percent share in 1993" (ibid.).

Consolidation of credit card debt is not the only way that HLTV lenders have gained market share. The cost savings of such lending have recently encouraged many mainstream mortgage lenders to extend HLTV mortgages in an original first lien to provide upfront liquidity for new homeowners (who might otherwise use credit cards for new home furnishings, which they might later refinance through a second-lien HLTV). Furthermore, as Fannie Mae and Freddie Mac look down-market for additional business, these A-minus–grade first-mortgage liens are quickly becoming accepted as an established business line.

As the HLTV niche encroaches on credit card and other consumer lending—and combines other creative developments, such as the portability of any excess liability across homes—some experts (including officials at the Department of Housing and Urban Development) expect the eventual development of so-called lifetime universal accounts that would combine credit card, automobile, mortgage, and other consumer debt with home equity borrowing and stock-brokerage sweep account technology, as well as portability. Such accounts may prove more efficient for borrowers and lenders than allocating credit through a series of discreet transactions. Ellen Roche of Freddie Mac asserted that "under a universal account arrangement, an array of assets—not just a house—would become the collateral for any loans taken out through the account" (1998, 24). The universal account process could ultimately bring the "efficiency of the mortgage-finance system to all consumer financing arrangements, lowering borrower costs in the process" (ibid., 28).

3

The Relationship between HLTV and Subprime Lending

HLTV Lending Defined

A small part of HLTV mortgage lending is geared toward subprime (high-risk) borrowers. For most HLTV borrowers, however, default risk is low. Lenders thus gain from increased assurance that loans will be repaid, while borrowers gain lower interest rates on their restructured credit card debt, plus tax-deductibility on some of their home equity loan interest.

The use of the word *subprime* to characterize HLTV lending has produced some confusion regarding its nature and risks and has led some observers to regard the practice as requiring specialized skills. In fact, the profitability and low average risk of HLTV lending have been among the industry's best-kept secrets. Some banks entering HLTV lending are surprised by the profitable low-risk lending opportunities it can offer. Banks like City Holding Company (Charleston, West Virginia) and Community West Bancshares (Goleta, California) are among those that until recently had been reluctant to enter the HLTV arena. After they began offering HLTV loans in 1997, bank executives soon realized that "the business is not as complex as they initially believed and is similar to the Title I lending they had done for years" (Talley 1998, 7).

The confusion has largely come from semantic difficulties. Before HLTV lending, the vast majority of loans outside the specifications of Fannie Mae and Freddie Mac went to borrowers with less than excellent credit. That is no longer the case, but the connection between failing to conform to Fannie Mae and Freddie Mac standards and subprime branding lives on. The subprime brand (or B and C ratings) is often still applied to all loans that have "been rejected by Freddie Mac or Fannie Mae because [the loans] don't meet their underwriting criteria" (Bush 1997, 34). Freddie Mac defines the subprime mortgage market as a

> niche that finances mortgages that do not meet traditional underwriting standards. Subprime mortgages are made to borrowers who have a variety of past credit problems of varying severity or to people with unconventional borrowing needs, including those that exceed 100 percent of the underlying property's value. (Roche 1998)

The implications of Freddie Mac's characterization are important: references to subprime mortgages may arise because of borrower characteristics or mortgage product characteristics. This confusion was evident in the November 1996 conflict between Greentree Financial, a leader in manufactured housing loans, and Faulkner & Gray, a publisher of industry statistics on the subprime lending industry. Before November 1996, Faulkner & Gray's *Inside B&C Lending* was reporting Greentree Financial as the number 2 servicer in B and C (or subprime) loans. "However, this ranking was based on the inclusion of [Greentree's] manufactured housing loans and Greentree did not want these loans to be reported as subprime. Consequently, its ranking fell to No. 28" (Froass 1997, 99).

The confusion has progressed to the point where the Mortgage Bankers Association of America now favors the term *nonconforming credit* for all such lending in this area.

With this distinction the MBA has cautioned that "a lender referred to as a home equity lender cannot [therefore] be assumed to lend solely to subprime borrowers." Even the term *nonconforming* can be confusing: HLTV loans fail to conform only to the *traditional* (rather than the current) standards set by government-sponsored enterprises such as Freddie Mac. Experts estimate that only about 30 percent of home equity mortgages are made to subprime borrowers (Froass 1997, 100). Furthermore, HLTV mortgages are generally A- to A-minus–grade credits and are categorized as nonconforming credits only because of their size relative to the value of mortgage collateral (which is only part of the lender's protection against default). The real protection enjoyed by lenders extends to the other assets and income of borrowers and to the nonpecuniary losses that borrowers would suffer from foreclosure.

Robert Grosser, chief executive, Cityscape Financial, commented that "there's a real misconception [regarding HLTV lending], because people marketing and selling these loans usually have a subprime division. It's not a subprime loan" (Timmons 1997a, 13). Similarly, industry leaders such as Gordon Monsen, formerly of Paine-Webber; Jeff Moore, chief executive of Mego Mortgage of Atlanta; and Dan Phillips, chief executive of FirstPlus Financial, insist that the HLTV business is not properly categorized as subprime lending (Bary 1997; Timmons 1997f; Muolo 1997).

The semantic confusion over subprime lending can also confound the discussion of the size of the HLTV industry. But whatever the definition of HLTV mortgage lending, its current market share remains small despite its recent growth. Industry sources have estimated that the entire nonconforming area (including both subprime and low-risk HLTV, as well as other nonconforming mortgages) accounts for 5–20 percent of the entire mortgage industry. At the end of 1996, nonconforming

loans made up approximately 9 percent of total outstanding mortgages and 11 percent of originations (see
tables 3–1 through 3–6 and figures 3–1 to 3–3). Around
56 percent of total nonconforming mortgage lending is
A-minus quality, another 25 percent B, 12 percent C,
and 5 percent D. Even if all nonconforming A-minus
loans were HLTV mortgages (which is certainly not the
case), HLTVs would at most comprise 5 percent of the
entire mortgage market. Direct estimates of the size of

TABLE 3–1
TOP SECURITIZERS OF HLTV LOANS, 1997

	Volume ($ millions)	Market Share (%)
FirstPlus Financial, Dallas[a]	3,559	37
Money Store, Sacramento[b]	1,202	12
Empire Funding, Austin	1,003	10
Master Financial, Orange	736	8
Cityscape Financial, Elmsford, New York[b]	609	6
Greentree, St. Paul[b]	507	5
National Bank of Keystone, West Virginia	500	5
Life Savings Bank, Riverside, California	474	5
PSB Lending, Carlsbad, California	415	4
Mego Mortgage, Atlanta[a]	322	3
Preferred Mortgage, Irvine, California	200	2
Direct Funding, Irvine, California	120	1

a. HLTV specialist
b. HLTV industry veteran
SOURCE: *National Mortgage News*, February 16, 1998, p. 44.

TABLE 3–2
SIZE OF NONCONFORMING MORTGAGE MARKET
RELATIVE TO TOTAL, DECEMBER 31, 1996
(in billions of dollars)

	Nonconforming	Total
Outstandings (cumulative)	$350	$3,900
Originations (annual)	$90	$785

SOURCE: Wahl and Focardi (1997).

TABLE 3–3
TOP TEN 125 PERCENT LOAN-TO-VALUE MORTGAGE
ORIGINATORS, FOURTH QUARTER, 1997

	Total Volume
FirstPlus Financial, Dallas	$1,168
Master Financial, Orange	278
PSB Lending Corp., Carlsbad, California	277
Preferred Mortgage, Irvine, California	250
Empire Funding, Austin	200
Mego Mortgage, Atlanta	170
NuMAX Mortgage Corp., Germantown, Maryland	147
N.F. Investments, Inc., Atlanta	100
PACE Funding, Dallas	29
Rock Financial Corp., Bingham Farms, Michigan	29

NOTE: 125 percent loan-to-value loans are intrinsically nonconforming because the borrowers do not have home values greater than 80 percent of the value of the loan and the loans are made outside special government programs such as those administered by the Federal Housing Administration and Title I.
SOURCE: *National Mortgage News*, March 23, 1998, p. 44.

TABLE 3–4
Top Ten Nonconforming Mortgage Wholesale Originators, Fourth Quarter, 1997

	Total Volume
Ford Consumer–Associates First, Irving, Texas	$1,090
FirstPlus Financial, Dallas	919
WMC Mortgage Company, Woodland Hills, California	692
Equicredit Corporation, Jacksonville	552
Option One Mortgage Corp., Santa Ana, California	515
Long Beach Mortgage, Orange	467
Household Financial Services, Prospect Heights, Illinois	400
Southern Pacific Funding Corp., Lake Oswego, Oregon	394
IMC Mortgage Company, Tampa	350
Money Store, Sacramento	344

NOTE: Wholesale originations provide a source of funds for other firms that make individual mortgage loans for their own portfolios.
SOURCE: *National Mortgage News,* March 23, 1998, p. 40.

the HLTV loan industry are quite a bit smaller than 5 percent. Industry experts such as Monsen pegged 1997 HLTV origination at slightly less than $10 billion of an overall residential origination market of $800 billion. That estimate puts HLTV lending at around 1.25 percent of the total mortgage market (Muolo 1997, 75).

HLTV Loan Customers and Marketing

One reason for confusion over the nature of subprime and HLTV lending is the use of similarly unconventional methods by both high-risk and low-risk HLTV lenders

TABLE 3–5
TOP TEN NONCONFORMING MORTGAGE CORRESPONDENT
ORIGINATORS, FOURTH QUARTER, 1997

	Total Volume
ContiMortgage Corp., Hatboro, Pennsylvania	$1,181
IMC Mortgage Company, Tampa	1,173
IMPAC Mortgage Holdings, Santa Ana Heights, California	900
AMRESCO Residential Credit Corp., Ontario, California	833
Residential Funding Corp./GMAC, Bloomington, Minnesota	700
Advanta Mortgage USA, Ft. Washington, Pennsylvania	664
Money Store, Sacramento	541
Greentree Financial, St. Paul	415
Equicredit Corporation, Jacksonville	314
United Companies Financial, Baton Rouge	273

NOTE: Correspondent originators are firms with a direct connection or friendly service relations with a lender. Correspondents typically originate loans for the lender's portfolio instead of their own and profit primarily from generating customers and processing loan applications.
SOURCE: *National Mortgage News,* March 23, 1998, p. 42.

to attract customers. "Just like the conforming mortgage business, there are three predominant distribution channels serving [nonconforming] lending—retail, wholesale, and correspondent" (Glass 1997, 65). Retail originators own their own distribution networks, while wholesalers rely primarily on brokers and correspondents to evaluate applicants and to approve loans. Brokers tend to be rather independent and sell originated loans to the highest bidding wholesaler. Correspondents, conversely, tend to partner with selected wholesalers.

TABLE 3–6
TOP TEN NONCONFORMING MORTGAGE RETAIL
ORIGINATORS, 1997

	Total Volume
Ford Consumer–Associates First, Irving	$3,400
Household Financial Services, Prospect Heights, Illinois	3,320
Commercial Credit–Travellers, Baltimore	2,156
Greentree Financial, St. Paul	2,154
Money Store, Sacramento	1,814
United Companies Financial, Baton Rouge	1,512
FirstPlus Financial, Dallas	1,170
IMC Mortgage Company, Tampa	890
Advanta Mortgage USA, Ft. Washington, Pennsylvania	864
FHB Funding Corp. Mineola, New York	760

NOTE: Retail originations are mortgage loans made by an institution for its own portfolio. Unlike wholesale originations, the funds for retail lending are generated internally through securitizations, equity and bond sales, and other primary means.
SOURCE: *National Mortgage News*, March 16, 1998, p. 1.

The retailers, wholesalers, brokers, and correspondents who distribute loans may be associated with traditional consumer finance companies, specialized nonconforming securitizers (*conduits*), or traditional mortgage banks (White and Levanthal 1997, 50). Chapter 2 described the beginnings of HLTV lending as a niche that was almost exclusively the purview of traditional finance companies. Over time HLTV lending has spread to specialized securitizers and most recently to traditional mortgage banks.

Within these companies has generally been a companion trend away from wholesale, arms-length lending toward direct retail lending and centralization. Two

FIGURE 3–1
PUBLIC ASSET-BACKED SECURITY ISSUANCE, BY SECTOR

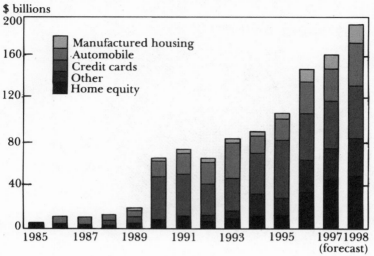

SOURCE: Flanagan, DiSerio, and Asato (1998).

FIGURE 3–2
HOME EQUITY ASSET-BACKED SECURITY ISSUANCE, BY PRODUCT TYPE

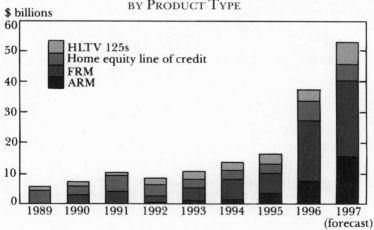

NOTE: FRM = fixed-rate mortgage; ARM = adjustable-rate mortgage.
SOURCE: Flanagan, DiSerio, and Asato (1998).

FIGURE 3–3
QUALITY COMPOSITION OF NONCONFORMING MORTGAGE DEBT

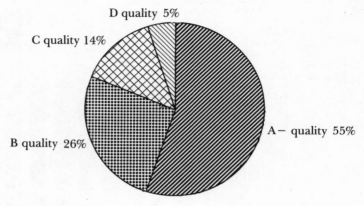

D quality 5%

C quality 14%

B quality 26%

A− quality 55%

SOURCE: White and Levanthal (1997).

complementary forces drive that trend. First, large, wholesale finance companies are quickly becoming obsolete, as mortgage conduits—specialized firms that do nothing but package and sell loans in secondary markets—become a cheaper and more efficient source of capital for brokers and correspondents. Second, as secondary markets become more competitive, brand capital becomes more important as an indicator of credit quality. Wholesale lenders such as FirstPlus and Mego Mortgage were some of the first to use their size (that is, economies of scale) and reputation to raise capital from those secondary markets. Although they may not need to build additional economies of scale to economize further on securitization, they are moving into retail origination to protect their brand-name capital in an increasingly competitive environment and to ensure a steady supply of loans to sell on the secondary market.

Because attrition rates are higher in the nonconforming lending process than in the conforming, non-conforming firms rely on mass marketing to generate lots of potential borrowers. Nonconforming loans require lengthy and detailed underwriting procedures but provide no guarantee that customers will like the final price offered and will accept the loans. Nonconforming lenders also need to employ adequate numbers of customer representatives and other staff; this situation requires higher origination expenses than one finds in conforming lending (Glass 1997, 68). Surveys indicate that the most common mass marketing vehicle used by nonconforming lenders is direct mail, followed by television advertising and telemarketing. Lenders also use radio and print advertising to generate new business, as well as internal retention systems for existing consumers (ibid., 65). First Fidelity Financial Corp. of Maryland, for example, estimates that it mails about 500,000 letters and calls more than 40,000 households each month soliciting HLTV customers.

Although the subprime and low-risk HLTV niches use similar channels, they market to distinct customer bases and employ different lending criteria, based on standard methods for determining borrower risk. All mortgage lending is traditionally based on the three Cs: collateral (LTV), character (credit history), and capacity (income to cover the mortgage and other debt). As discussed, HLTV lenders discovered during the recession in the early 1990s that character and capacity can often overshadow collateral in importance, a lesson that other consumer lenders learned long ago. Rating agencies such as Standard & Poor's, Moody's, Fitch IBCA, and Duff & Phelps agree that "the borrower's willingness and ability to service the loan, as measured by credit scores" are at least as critical to loan quality as collateral as measured by LTV (Fitch Investors Service 1997, 3; Willis-Boyland 1997, 29; Fitch IBCA 1998b, 3). In fact, as early as December 1996, Fitch IBCA—one of the most sophisticated rating agencies in its approach to subprime lending—concluded that a borrower's credit standing is the most important driver of default probability (Fitch Investors Service 1996b).

Mortgage professionals, including those at Freddie Mac, agree that the credit scores relied on by HLTV lenders and the consumer credit industry are excellent measures of the borrower's credit standing and ultimate loan performance (Freddie Mac 1997). As Fitch IBCA (1998b, 3) explains,

> credit scoring is a mechanism for uniformly assessing borrowers by assigning numerical values to various borrower attributes that have been observed to positively or negatively correlate with credit behavior. . . . Credit scores are generated by three major repositories: Experian, TransUnion, and Equifax. Each repository score was designed by Fair Isaac and has comparable scales, with 900 being the highest.

In recent years, credit scoring technology has been extended beyond simple forecasting of default risk to forecasting bankruptcy, repayment rates, and even post–default collection amounts and individual collection agency performance. (In the following text, *credit scoring* is referred to narrowly as the measurement of default risk.)

Opportunities in subprime lending often result from lenders' willingness to look beyond mere credit scores: some consumers are better credit risks than their scores indicate, and firms willing to dig deeper to find such consumers can unearth profitable low-risk opportunities.

While not the only ingredient in market estimates of credit quality, FICO scores (credit scores developed by Fair Isaac and Company) provide a useful measure for quantifying default risk. In general, first-trust mortgage borrowers with FICO scores above 660 are considered to have a good credit reputation. Borrowers with FICO scores between 660 and 620 are somewhat riskier borrowers, for whom underwriters should perform a more extensive review. Borrowers with scores below 620 should be subjected to a thorough, cautious review (Freddie Mac 1997, 2). The market generally considers any borrower with a credit score above 620 as a prime candidate for a mortgage. These borrowers are considered of A quality. Those with scores ranging from 580 to 620 are generally considered A-minus quality. Those below 580 are generally considered B- and C-quality (subprime) borrowers. Individuals can be rated less than 580 simply because they do not have a verifiable source of income—for example, if they are self-employed or make most of their earnings on commission. Those individuals cannot avoid a low score even if they have low debt-to-income ratios. Such borrowers are the mainstay of the subprime lending industry.

Of course, FICO credit scores apply to the borrower rather than the loan; some adjustment must be made when using these scores to compare the credit risk of first (senior) mortgages and second (junior) mortgages. Credit standards based on FICO scores for first-mortgage products are different from those for second mortgages, and most HLTV loans are second mortgages. Although underwriting standards vary and depend on qualitative factors other than FICO scores (and credit risks for first mortgages also depend on the loan-to-value ratio of the first mortgage), the approximate cutoff for a prime HLTV second-trust borrower is apparently 40 FICO points higher than for a first-trust customer (within the relevant range of scores). That is, the default risk of a typical HLTV loan with a FICO score of 660 is roughly comparable with that of a typical first-trust mortgage with a FICO score of 620.

Actual HLTV borrowers tend to have high FICO scores and to qualify as prime borrowers. HLTV borrowers exhibit weighted average credit scores in the 670–680 range. "Only borrowers with high credit scores are eligible for [HLTV] loans," according to Paul Jenison, managing director, PaineWebber, Inc., an active investor in HLTV securities. The borrower who cannot get a loan that qualifies for sale to a secondary mortgage agency is "not going to be able to get a high LTV loan" (Timmons 1997k). In September 1997, FirstPlus Financial reported an average FICO score of 684, according to "FirstPlus Reports Net Rose 271 percent in Quarter," *American Banker*, November 3, 1997. Stuart-Wright Mortgage, Inc., of LaPalma, California, boasted an average score of 700 (Timmons 1997g).

The high quality of HLTV portfolios is reflected in a comparison of HLTV credit scores to averages for the conforming mortgage industry and government mortgage programs, even after adjusting for the difference between first- and second-trust mortgages. Table 3–7 provides data on the distribution of credit scores for conventional, government, and FirstPlus HLTV loan securitizations for 1997. In that year 93.3 percent of conventional loans had credit scores above 620. In contrast 70.3 percent of government mortgage loan obligations—that is, those extended through the Government National Mortgage Association and other assistance programs—and 55 percent of nonconforming loans of all kinds (see figure 3–3) had credit scores greater than 620. Virtually all the loans included in the FirstPlus Home Loan Owner Trust Series 1997–4 portfolio had scores above 620—76.79 percent, in fact, had credit scores greater than 660 (Fitch IBCA 1998a, 4). Only 3.2 percent of conventional loans were made to borrowers with credit scores in the 600–619 B range, while 10.4 percent of government loans and 26 percent of nonconforming loans were made to borrowers in this category. Only 2.0 percent and 1.6 percent of conventional loans were made to borrowers in the 580–599 C and less than

TABLE 3–7

DISTRIBUTION OF MORTGAGE LOANS BY CREDIT SCORE
RANGE AND LOAN TYPE, 1997 ORIGINATIONS
(in percent)

	Conventional Average[a]	Government Average[a]	FirstPlus 125s[b]
>620	93.30	70.30	99.66
600–619	3.20	10.40	0.33
580–599	2.00	8.20	0.00
<580	1.60	11.20	0.00

Distribution above 620

	All Mortgages	VA	FHA	FirstPlus 125s
>720	57.51	51.94	46.83	13.98
680–719	16.11	16.14	19.02	39.11
660–679	6.41	6.77	7.53	23.70
640–659	5.01	6.22	6.60	17.70
620–639	3.91	5.01	5.32	5.17
<619[a]	11.05	13.92	14.70	0.34

a. Government loans are all those issued through subsidized programs such as FHA, VA, and GNMA. Conventional loans are conforming loans issued outside special government programs.
b. The FirstPlus pool only includes loans with FICO credit scores greater than 600. Source: Fitch IBCA. 1998. *FirstPlus Home Loan Owner Trust Series 1997–4.* New York: Fitch IBCA, January 29, p. 4.
SOURCE: For a, Wahl, Matthew, and Focardi (1997); for b, Fitch IBCA (1998); for all mortgages, VA, and FHA, Fair Isaac and Co.

580 D ranges, respectively, while 8.2 percent and 11.2 percent of government loans and 14 percent and 5 percent of nonconforming loans were made to individuals in these categories.

These numbers suggest that a high percentage of government loans have subprime borrower characteristics. Furthermore, FirstPlus's HLTV loan quality lies somewhere between the average quality of subprime loans and the quality of conforming loans; it probably exceeds the average quality of loans extended through established government programs (Wahl and Focardi 1997, 34).

HLTV loan quality generally has been characterized as lying "somewhere between a pure unsecured loan—like a credit card—and a traditional second mortgage" (Flanagan, DiSerio, and Asato 1998, 49), given that "defaults are rarer on second mortgages than on unsecured credit card loans," ostensibly because consumers do not face the same incentives to default on mortgages (Clark 1998, 38). According to Jonathan Lieberman, an analyst at Moody's Investors Service, HLTV debts are no riskier than credit card loans (Timmons 1997c). Another analyst observed that "in a recession FirstPlus probably won't do any worse than credit card companies—and no one's launching a Senate investigation of them." Further, "most [HLTV] issuers target high FICO (credit score) borrowers who have demonstrated the ability to use and manage credit, as little or no value is placed on the collateral" (Clark 1998, 38). Even loans to subprime customers usually have sufficient collateral to offset the credit risk.

As with credit card lending, HLTV loan underwriters do not place much value on being repaid by any underlying collateral; therefore, HLTV lenders usually extend these loans only to customers with high credit scores and sufficient income. Timothy J. O'Neill, Jr., senior vice president, First Indiana Bank, Indianapolis, characterized the typical HLTV borrower as an individual who "has a family and a good credit history, but increased debt resulting from medical bills, credit cards, short-term installment debt, or education costs" (Brockman 1998, 9). Fitch IBCA's research has established that the attributes of [HLTV] borrowers are reflective of 'A'–'A-minus' borrowers. The weighted average credit score falls in the 670–680 range, the average age is in the late 30s to early 40s, residency is established for an average of four to five years, and borrowers are employed in the same position for five years or more. In addition, household income averages about $60,000 with some portfolios in the $70,000 range. Most pools consist primarily (95 percent–97 percent) of salaried versus self-employed borrowers, with back-end debt-to-income ratios after the [HLTV] loan of 35 percent to 40 percent. [These] attributes compare favorably to the respective attributes for subprime port-folios. Credit scores for 'A-minus'/'B' subprime pools tend to average in the high 500 to low 600 range and median household income for all subprime borrowers is approximately $34,000. In addition, subprime bor-rowers have, on average, less than two years in their current residence or occupation. (1998b, 3)

These characterizations based on credit score com-parisons may underestimate the relative quality of HLTV loans. HLTV lenders charge lower interest rates on their credits, as noted, because they believe that link-ing debt to the consumer's home discourages voluntary default. Credit card loans do not enjoy that same protec-tion.

Some skeptics maintain that HLTV borrowers start out looking sound but are prone to subprime default characteristics later because of poor credit habits and the high LTV leverage. Although the HLTV market has not yet been tested through a cyclical downturn, this assess-ment is questionable. Lenders'

performance and experience in other related areas, such as FHA Title I loans, consumer loans, credit cards, or other types of mortgages can help to mitigate the lack of direct historical experience. . . . Loan performance of [HLTV] versus conventional home equity securitizations shows that, in the first six months, average home equity delinquencies are four to five times greater than comparable [HLTV] delinquencies. (Fitch IBCA 1998b, 7)

Table 3–8 shows that delinquency rates on HLTV loans have been extremely modest, even in the face of record defaults on credit card debt. As of December 1997, Fitch IBCA (1998b, 4) reported that "90-day plus delinquencies of traditional home equity pools are approximately four to five times greater" than those of

TABLE 3–8

AVERAGE SIX-MONTH LOSSES AND DELINQUENCIES FOR FIXED-RATE HOME-EQUITY LOAN AND HIGH LOAN-TO-VALUE (HLTV) HOME EQUITY LOAN SECURITIZATIONS, DECEMBER 1997

	Home Equity	HLTV
Original balance	588,775,587	427,300,820
Delinquency (%)		
30 days	3.51	0.89
60 days	1.19	0.36
90 days	1.47	0.59
Foreclosure	1.41	0.00
Real estate owned	0.17	0.00
90+ days	3.04	0.59
Cumulative losses ($)	66,354	273,848
As % of original	0.01	0.06

NOTE: Home equity loans typically result in a loan-to-value ratio of less than 100 percent although the LTV may exceed 100 percent under certain subsidized programs such as Title I. The proceeds of such loans are usually required to be applied toward home improvement or, more recently, debt consolidation. High loan-to-value loans may reach ratios of up to 125 percent. The proceeds may be used for any purpose the borrower desires.
SOURCE: Fitch IBCA (1998).

HLTV mortgage loans. Fitch IBCA showed higher cumulative losses on HLTV loans during the same period but attributed that to differences in accounting conventions: HLTV lenders write off 100 percent of their loans six months after default (a more conservative accounting standard more like the treatment of credit card loans than mortgage loans) rather than estimating some recovery value and keeping the loans on the books. Home equity pools, in contrast, write off losses only after they are realized, and delinquent loans that are refinanced are not treated as charge-offs.

Even in the truly subprime market, where delinquency and foreclosure rates are higher than in the low-risk HLTV market, credit scoring and market discipline (coming from external funding sources) should ensure that interest rates are set high enough to provide adequate expected return to offset credit risk. Thus, attributing high delinquencies to lax underwriting standards, even in the subprime market, misstates the relevant issue: whether the loan is priced correctly. Sound underwriting takes into account not only default risk but the relationship of default risk to the price of the loan. In this light, higher default rates may indicate nothing more than expanded access to credit (the so-called democratization of finance) that legislators and regulators have pushed for since the early days of the Community Reinvestment Act (Wahl and Focardi 1997, 34). (For a discussion of recent controversies regarding the risks of subprime home equity lending, see Prakash [1998.])

In summary, HLTV loans cater primarily to high-quality (A or A− rated) credit risks. Any judgment of the soundness of underwriting standards should take into account not only the default characteristics of their borrowers but the relationship between default probability (or other risks) and loan cost. Experts believe that the trend toward risk-based pricing should lessen bimodal categorizations between conforming and nonconforming (or prime and subprime) borrowing in favor of a more continuous classification of borrowers that identifies both the level of risk and the appropriate return for bearing that risk (Wahl and Focardi 1997, 36).

4
A Profile of the Industry

What Institutions Make HLTV Loans?

The HLTV industry is made up of a variety of intermediaries, including consumer finance companies, specialized nonconforming securitizers, and traditional mortgage banks. Consumer finance companies specializing in HLTV lending include firms such as the FirstPlus Financial Group of Texas. Other traditional consumer finance companies active in HLTVs, but not considered specialists, include the Money Store (New Jersey), United Companies Financial Corporation (Louisiana), and Greentree Financial (Minnesota). FirstPlus Financial is the largest of the HLTV securitizers; the firm originates, purchases, and services HLTV loans.

Other firms supplying HLTV credit include specialized HLTV securitizers. These firms merely provide funding conduits for other companies that originate, purchase, or service loans. These securitizers may be independent firms or subsidiaries of other mortgage companies. In general, they are analogous to a contemporary incarnation of wholesale mortgage company finance. Because securitized loan pools tend to be large, such firms rarely specialize in a particular niche. Firms such as Residential Funding Corporation (a General Motors Acceptance Corporation subsidiary) and Contifinancial Corporation (New York) are examples of independent conduits. Empire Funding, associated with Empire Financial Corporation, is an example of a conduit owned by a mortgage–consumer finance firm.

More recently, traditional mortgage banks, savings and loans, credit unions, and other institutions have begun to offer HLTV products. Mego Mortgage Corporation (Georgia) and Countrywide Home Loans (California) are examples of mortgage companies that have offered HLTV loans for some time. Other traditional financial intermediaries that now offer HLTV loans are numerous. Although the multitude of firms now offering HLTV loans is a disparate group, they all share the desire to expand their menu of loan products and the ability to use securitization to finance loans as reported in "B&C Market Posts Record Year in '97," *Inside B&C Lending,* January 19, 1998.

The continued viability of HLTV lending as it is currently financed depends on the continuation of market demand for the asset-backed securities offered by HLTV intermediaries. That source of funding depends in turn on the fundamental performance of the securities themselves in conjunction with overall economic conditions.

Securitization as a Source of Market Growth

HLTV loans are typically securitized and sold to investors rather than held in the loan portfolios of the originators (Brockman 1998, 9). "FirstPlus wasn't the first company to make [HLTV] loans. But it was the first to bring the product to Wall Street, in an asset-backed-securities deal with Bank One Capital Corp. in late 1994. The move opened the market and earned [FirstPlus CEO Dan Phillips] a number of fans." (See Timmons [1997i] for additional information on the role of FirstPlus in developing the HLTV industry.)

Securitization entails the pooling of large numbers of loans to provide statistically predictable average loan performance. Only firms that can originate or purchase enough loans to construct a pool of $100 million or more can structure a deal. Smaller institutions, however, are not entirely locked out of this market. Smaller banks that have good loan volumes but not the legal staff or investment banking resources to handle a public issue can still securitize loans through the private placement market. In this way the smaller institutions avoid the expensive and time-consuming tasks of registering the securities with regulators and preparing disclosure forms. Although the resulting securities are exclusively the domain of large institutional investors, this situation does not seem to have stifled opportunities over the past several years. According to Steven J. Day, chief executive, City Holding (Charleston, West Virginia), his bank has had little trouble lining up buyers for its private placements (Talley 1998). First Indiana Bank of Indianapolis has been selling an average of $13 million worth of HLTV loans each month since it began offering the product in August 1997 (Brockman 1998).

Within both these channels, more than $8.75 billion worth of HLTV loans were securitized in 1997. Peter Rubenstein, senior vice president, PaineWebber, Inc., expects that number almost to double in 1998 (Timmons 1998d). Despite the dramatic growth of HLTV loans, their asset-backed securities still represented less than 5 percent of securitized assets issued during 1997. That percentage is likely to grow as the HLTV industry continues to expand and to absorb market share from other forms of consumer credit.

Because securitization is a common form of finance in the traditional mortgage and credit card industries, the participation of HLTV lending—which combines elements of both—in the securitization boom is not surprising. Securitization has expanded to include securities that had been excluded from the market.

Part of the expansion in the range of loans securitized has been made possible by fundamental changes in the technology of rating credit and by the role of the rating agencies in providing standards and ratings for both the HLTV and subprime industries. In 1996, Standard & Poor's rated around 98 percent of all nonconforming securitizations by dollar value and 95 percent by number. The majority of these deals were issued as *wraps*, that is, asset-backed securities whose quality is wrapped or enhanced by a monoline (specialist) insurer. Standard & Poor's and Moody's exclusively rated the monoline insurers. Since a deal can only get the highest rating of its weakest link, Standard & Poor's and Moody's effectively held a virtual duopoly over the nonconforming securities market until 1997 (Willis-Boyland 1997, 32).

The monoline insurers are subject to certain exposure limits to different credit types, however, and these limits have recently become binding on the nonconforming mortgage loan industry. Therefore, nonconforming mortgage securitizations have recently taken the form of senior-subordinate deals (described below). In fact, most deals issued in 1997 had senior-subordinate structures. The attraction of this segmentation of risk is that senior (collateralized) debts appeal to investors with limited taste for risk or limited ability to understand the risks of the underlying loans.

That change in the structure of securitizations has also encouraged new entry by rating agencies. Standard & Poor's and Moody's do not enjoy the same duopoly over the senior-subordinate deals as they do over wraps: Fitch IBCA and Duff & Phelps specialize in senior-subordinate deals, with Fitch IBCA the top rating agency in such structures.

Another important development will expand the securitization capability of the industry—the involvement of Freddie Mac and Fannie Mae in securitizing nonconforming mortgages. Although these two agencies were expected to securitize only about $2.5 billion in nonconforming loans during all 1997, the credits that they would take are all in the A-minus range, which may place them in direct competition with existing securitizers of nonconforming mortgages as reported in "Freddie Mac and Fannie Mae Stay Active, " *Inside B&C Lending*, September 1, 1997 (see also White and Levanthal [1997, 50]).

Securitization Structure and Risk

Securitization became a popular funding source in the 1980s for a variety of reasons. First, a change in tax laws permitted "the tax-free pass through of cash flows from home loans to mortgage securities, thereby avoiding double taxation" (Kendall 1996, 6). Second, the modernization of investment powers of institutional investors under the Employee Retirement Income Security Act permitted them to hold asset-backed securities in their portfolio. Third, companies could use cheap computing power to estimate and to track pool performance, to run options pricing models, to keep track of payments from the pool, and to pass coupons through to investors (ibid.).

Although these three factors were largely in place at the end of the 1970s, securitization did not catch on until the late 1980s. This lag reflected the fact that financial institutions faced rising capital standards and increasing scarcity of capital during the 1980s, which raised the cost of on–balance-sheet finance. Furthermore, the popularity of securitization grew with its use as a liquidation tool of the Resolution Trust Corporation. Leon Kendall, professor of finance, Northwestern University, lists seven basic requirements for securitization: standardized contracts, the grading of risk through underwriting, a database of historical statistics, the standardization of applicable laws, the standardization of servicer quality, a reliable supply of quality credit enhancers, and computers to handle the complexity of the analysis. As long as legal claims are understood regarding a large pool of standard financial contracts with estimable performance and credible backing, securitizers can pool the contracts and sell securities against claims on the pool (ibid., 7).

Securitizers do exactly this. Suppose that a lender has a pool of mortgages. If all payments are made according to plan, they all amortize like the one in figure 4–1. Rarely, however, are all payments made according to plan across a pool of several thousand mortgages. Borrowers may default; this action leads to chargeoffs. Interest rates may fall: resulting refinancings will be reflected in early payoffs. The average life of the mortgages in the pool, therefore, will almost certainly not be the planned thirty years.

Much research has focused on estimating the size and timing of actual prepayments and repayments of loan principal. This statistical research has resulted in the Public Securities Association model of principal

FIGURE 4–1

AMORTIZATION OF PRINCIPAL PAYMENTS ON A THIRTY-YEAR, $10,000 MORTGAGE AT 9.5 PERCENT, NO PREPAYMENT

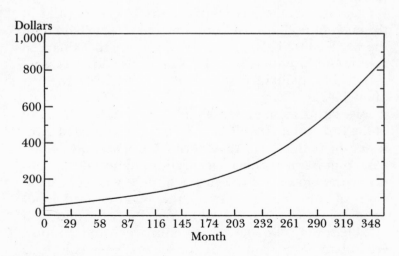

SOURCE: Kendall (1996).

flows. Figure 4–2 depicts the average principal payoff behavior of a hypothetical loan pool.

PSA prepayment speed is a measure of the rate of prepayment of mortgage loans developed by the Public Securities Association, the national trade association of banks, dealers, and brokers that underwrite, trade, and distribute mortgage-backed securities, U.S. government and federal agency securities, and municipal securities. This model represents an assumed rate of prepayment each month of the outstanding principal balance of a pool of new mortgage loans. The baseline PSA model (which represents past experience for all mortgage originations) assumes initial prepayment rates of 0.2 percent per annum of the principal mortgage balance in the first month after origination and an increase of an additional 0.2 percent per annum in each month thereafter (for example, 0.4 percent per annum in the second month)

FIGURE 4–2

AVERAGE AMORTIZATION OF PRINCIPAL PAYMENTS ON A
THIRTY-YEAR, $10,000 MORTGAGE AT 9.5 PERCENT,
160 PERCENT OF PSA ESTIMATED PREPAYMENT MODEL

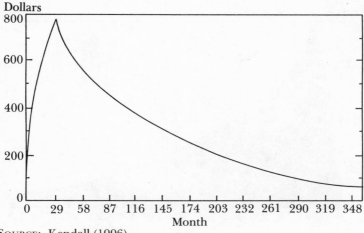

SOURCE: Kendall (1996).

41

until the thirtieth month. Beginning in the thirtieth month and in each month thereafter, the baseline model assumes a constant annual prepayment rate (CPR) of 6 percent. Variations in the baseline model are calculated as multiples of this rate path. A 150 percent PSA, for example, assumes annual prepayment rates will be 0.3 percent in month one and 0.6 percent in month two, will reach 9 percent in month thirty, and will remain constant at 9 percent thereafter. A PSA of 0 percent assumes no prepayments. The 160 percent PSA illustrated is representative of the (conservative) assumptions used in mortgage securitizations.

Figure 4–3 simply breaks this expected behavior into segmented claims that can be sold on securities markets. The first segment, or tranche, receives all principal payments in the early years and is paid off in forty-eight months. The second segment then begins to receive pay-

FIGURE 4–3
FOUR-CLASS SEQUENTIAL COLLATERALIZED MORTGAGE
OBLIGATION PRINCIPAL PAYMENTS, 160 PERCENT
OF PSA ESTIMATED PREPAYMENT MODEL

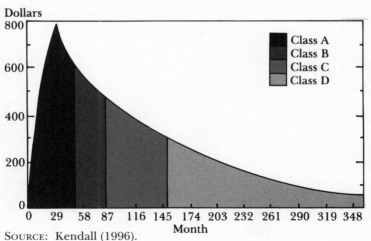

SOURCE: Kendall (1996).

ments and is paid off in the eighty-fourth month, and so on. The effects of unexpected defaults or prepayments are distributed across the segments according to the individual contract, with the originating institution taking responsibility for the residual gain or loss. The longer investors in the lower segments must wait for their returns, the more risky those returns may be. If unexpected defaults or prepayments get too large in some kinds of securitizations (notably, credit card deals), the deal is cancelled, and investors are immediately repaid in what is commonly referred to as an early amortization.

The example of a senior-subordinate securitization is quite simple. In practice, securitizations can have more than fifty segments, including those for interest-only strips, principal-only strips, and other varied characteristics. The goal of this customization is to meet a variety of investor preferences for different types of securities. But the seven basic requirements for a successful securitization remain constant no matter how many tranches or fancy payment categories are included. In general, therefore, the main sources of risk for investors and issuers of such securities also remain the same.

The main source of risk in the HLTV market today is probably model risk, which is the underwriter's ability to predict default and prepayment behavior accurately over the life of the contract. The key components of model risk at issue are the seasoning of the loans included in the pool (which is directly related to the depth of historical background on the underlying financial contracts—in the present case, HLTV mortgage loans), unexpected defaults, and unexpected prepayments.

Seasoning relates to both the length of time that loans have been outstanding before inclusion in the pool and the maturity of the market for particular financial contracts. If the market for a particular financial contract, such as HLTV mortgage loans, is relatively young, most financial contracts of that type would also be relatively unseasoned. There is considerable debate about the degree to which the HLTV loan market, and the loans themselves, are unseasoned. In general, nonconforming loans are much younger than conforming loans. Wahl and Focardi (1997, 31) report that as of May 1997 "60 percent of first-lien [nonconforming] loans outstanding were made in 1996 or the early part of 1997, compared with only a 17 percent share of [conforming] loans."

Although the nonconforming mortgage industry is relatively young, the HLTV sector has its origins in Title I lending. Some of the first HLTV securitizations were constructed with assumptions based almost entirely on Title I loan performance. To demonstrate expected performance for its first securitizations—which were also the first HLTV loans ever securitized—FirstPlus relied extensively on Title I performance data. According to Dan Phillips, chief executive officer of FirstPlus, "that's how we got the rating agencies to rate the loans, and the insurers to insure them" (Timmons 1996). Investors and underwriters have far more performance data with HLTVs now than in late 1994, when Phillips's first securitization went to market, but performance expectations are still treated gingerly by rating agencies since long-term behavior is relatively unknown (Fitch IBCA 1998b, 6).

Default risk is central to pricing asset-backed securities. Securitizations are structured in such a way that the returns to investors are expected to be reasonable as long as the pool of loans behaves in the manner predicted by the underwriters' economic models; that is, as long as defaults and prepayments remain within certain bounds. If defaults or prepayments rise above certain limits (which vary with each individual contract), principal or interest payments may not be sufficient to meet the obligations of the issuer. If that happens, the pool will be liquidated prior to its stated maturity in an early amortization. Therefore, the viability of any particular offer relies critically on the bounds set for defaults and prepayments and their balance against investor yield. But the *unexpected* level of defaults or prepayments, rather than their absolute level, can undermine the success of the asset-backed security offering.

Prepayment risk is another factor affecting the returns to asset-backed securities. Although HLTV pools have performed above the default expectations for most models, there is substantial concern and debate about prepayment rates. Investor concern arises because prepayment and a resulting early amortization are more likely in a low–interest rate environment (because low interest rates make refinancing attractive to the borrower). Suppose that the investor holds securities paying a coupon rate of 10 percent. If interest rates drop to 8 percent and borrowers refinance, early amortization will mean that the investor's return will fall to 8 percent. With residential mortgages, the propensity to prepay is much higher when interest rates fall; this situation can present substantial risk to investors. The extremely low–interest rate environment of 1997, for example, is generally expected to continue throughout 1998 and lead to further refinancing activity (Kochen 1996, 112–13).

Prepayment risk tends to be lower for HLTV mortgage loans than for conforming A credits. Jeff Moore, president, Mego Mortgage (Atlanta), maintains that "because the borrower ends up with a loan-to-value on the property in excess of 100 percent, they usually stay in the loan for some time because they can't quickly refinance out and they still have relatively high debt ratios" (Hewitt 1997, 177).

Investors have been satisfied with the general performance of HLTV loan securitizations largely because the model risk has been treated rather conservatively and credit enhancements protecting asset-backed securities holders have consequently been more than adequate. Fitch IBCA (1998b, 6) reports that "typical

[HLTV] credit enhancement levels indicate that the 'AAA' tranche could withstand gross losses of 30 percent–40 percent of the pool. This is approximately three to four times greater than the losses implied by 'AAA' credit enhancement levels for a typical subprime pool." (See also "PaineWebber Senior Vice President Profiles the 125 Percent LTV Sector," *National Mortgage News*, March 23, 1998.) HLTV securitizations "have self-regulated credit support," according to Peter Rubenstein, PaineWebber senior vice president. "The securitized pools of [HLTV] loans peddled on Wall Street contain a sizable amount of excess spread and overcollateralization, which act as a cushion if the loans do not perform as expected" (Timmons 1998d). While such support seems high for a mortgage securitization, in fact the terms of these securitizations are much like those of credit cards (Fitch IBCA 1998b; Fitch Investors Service 1996a).

5
Risk and the Social Costs and Benefits of HLTV Lending

The previous chapters pointed out that because the HLTV industry is relatively young, there is often confusion over the nature of HLTV lending, its customers, and suppliers. Similar misunderstandings surround the potential risks and the related social costs and benefits that HLTV lending poses to individuals, issuers, and the economy. This chapter addresses some of these popular misconceptions in light of economic theory and empirical evidence.

Risk Reduction from HLTV Lending

As shown, benefits of HLTV lending accrue to consumers, who enjoy lower costs of credit because (1) HLTV lending allows them to commit to avoiding default voluntarily on their consumer loans and (2) because the diversified funding sources used by HLTV lenders limit interest rate risk associated with volatility of funding cost. Benefits from these two influences also accrue to the economy as a whole since lower interest costs, lower interest rate risk, and lower probabilities of consumer default make the financial system more stable and thus less likely to magnify shocks that originate elsewhere in the economy (see Calomiris [1995] for a review of the literature on financial fragility).

Securitization broadens the financial industry's capital base to securities investors worldwide. This concept, generally referred to as capital deepening, has been credited with ameliorating the effects of the U.S. recession in the early 1990s. Sources of funds in foreign countries that were not experiencing recessions during the early 1990s (especially Japan) established a sizable presence in the United States during this period. Although the presence of foreign banks augmented lending by domestic banks, foreign banks did not only lend directly to U.S. firms. They often supplied funds through U.S. banks—which ostensibly had better information about U.S. borrowers—through commercial loan participations and whole commercial loan purchases. In this manner foreign banks contributed additional capital to U.S. credit markets when shortages would have otherwise constrained lending more severely. This capital-deepening effect mitigated the credit channel effect of the recession and promoted a shallower downturn and quicker recovery than would otherwise have been the case (Calomiris and Carey 1994; Nolle 1995; DeYoung and Nolle 1995; Goldberg 1992; Goldberg and Saunders 1981).

Because "an increasing share of the investor market for mortgage securities is overseas" (Korell 1996, 97), the securitization of conforming, subprime, and HLTV lending contributes to this capital deepening. Foreign investment activity in HLTV securitizations therefore helps stabilize the U.S. economy by providing more robust financing alternatives that do not rely entirely on the performance of the domestic capital market.

Is there is a dark side to securitization? Might securitization expose consumer financing costs to a new risk—the possibility that funding might be withdrawn suddenly from the market? The possibility of a significant interruption is remote. Securitized debt is held by diverse and sophisticated market participants, and the structure of these securitization conduits is customized to cater to the preferences and concerns of those securities holders. Multiple safeguards are built into the structure of securitized debt to protect debtholders and thus to limit their incentive to flee in response to heightened risk. Experienced investors understand how to measure and to manage the risks of HLTV, while rating agencies provide detailed information on securitizations, asset quality, collateral, and other factors. The fundamental characteristics of both HLTV and subprime lending are now well understood, as evidenced by the recent entrance of Fannie Mae and Freddie Mac to these arenas.

In addition to reducing both the risk of consumer default and the volatility of the cost of consumer credit, HLTV lending also enables consumers to liquefy the value of their home equity in times of recession—in effect to maintain smooth consumption during fluctuations in income. Just as firms benefited from the greater financial flexibility afforded by expanded opportunities in bond markets in the late 1980s, consumers benefit from the ability to convert illiquid home equity (and good credit reputations) into quick cash. Without HLTV lending during the recession of the early 1990s, many consumers experienced significant increases in their LTVs as economic devaluations reduced home values. Caplin, Freeman, and Tracey used data from the early 1990s recession to establish that

> when adverse economic shocks cause property values in a region to decrease, the damage to collateral makes it difficult or impossible for some homeowners to obtain new mortgages. . . . In regions suffering from adverse economic conditions, the ability to refinance will likely be constrained by declining property values. As LTVs increase into the 80–90 percent region, the costs of refinancing increase due to the need for [private mortgage insurance]. As LTVs increase past 90 percent, homeowners may be completely rationed out of the refinance market. . . . This inability to refinance has further economic impacts on the region through lowering the wealth and the discretionary income of

49

the local homeowners, thereby deepening the regional recession (1997, 496, 498–99)

when consumers reduce spending because of liquidity
pressures or personal bankruptcy. The authors' findings
therefore suggest that HLTV lending can help households weather the effects of recessions and can significantly stabilize shocks to aggregate demand that would
otherwise have more severe effects on the economy.

Reloading and Churning

Detractors of HLTV lending maintain that consumers
have several methods of abusing the new credit opportunities. According to these critics, some consumers who
consolidate debts in an HLTV loan respond to their
lower payments by increasing their borrowings from
credit cards and other sources, a form of behavior
termed *reloading*. A related problem is so-called *churning*,
whereby borrowers pay down credit card debt with an
unreported HLTV loan, then trick other lenders into
granting a second, larger HLTV loan on even better
terms.

To the extent that reloading and churning are nei-
ther anticipated nor prevented by lenders, they are dis-
equilibrium phenomena that depend on irrational
decision making by either banks or consumers. Disequi-
librium churning and reloading would be largely absent
in a rational lending process, one in which lenders understand risk (including the risk of fraud) and protect
themselves accordingly, and in which consumers understand the incentives to limit their default risk. Rational
HLTV lenders—and other providers of consumer
credit—obtain and analyze a wealth of data to determine
the risk of lending to loan applicants. Presumably, lending standards—enforced by managerial incentives, rating agency oversight, and market discipline—would not

reward (or permit) consumers to trick lenders systematically.

In fact HLTV lenders explicitly guard against reloading and churning. Even if borrowers meet HLTV underwriting guidelines, the amount of cash that the borrower can obtain beyond that required for debt consolidation is small (less than $5,000) for all but those with the best credit scores (more than 660 for FirstPlus Financial Group, Inc.) (FirstPlus Financial Group 1997). Lenders also have begun to adjust for potential churning by applying stricter credit standards to applicants with pre-existing junior-lien debt-consolidation activity not yet reflected in their credit reports, according to "Better Prepays on High LTV Mortgages Expected in 1998," *Inside B&C Lending*, March 2, 1998 (see also Fitch IBCA [1998b]). FirstPlus, for example, raises the credit-score cutoff for its borrowers if the borrowers have a second-lien mortgage. To guard against HLTV loans that may be hidden from credit records, lenders also check consumers' records to see if credit card debt has recently been paid down—a potential indicator of an attempt to churn.

Rational HLTV borrowers also understand that by entering into an HLTV contract they are reducing the benefits of declaring bankruptcy. That action should provide a powerful disincentive to excessive reloading or churning since the HLTV borrower bears a greater share of the cost from taking on excessive debt than if borrowing only on noncollateralized credit cards. The security of collateral not only induces lenders to charge lower interest rates but also reduces financial fragility among borrowers by discouraging default and by encouraging them to maintain less debt. Furthermore, nothing about HLTV lending per se increases the debt service burdens of *unwise* consumers (those who do not respond properly to economic incentives to limit risk). Credit cards and other consumer loans already suffice for those who are determined to behave imprudently (Timmons 1997h; Fitch IBCA 1998b).

But we are *not* arguing that the credit card balances of a rational consumer should remain at zero after a borrower obtains an HLTV loan. Rational consumers have good reasons to combine HLTV borrowing with credit card borrowing and even to reload to some extent after consolidating their credit card debts through an HLTV loan.

Consider the example of thirty-five-year-old parents of a family of four with combined annual income of $80,000. College graduates, both expect their income to grow rapidly over the next decade. The risk of a decline in their income is small. The value of their home is $200,000, and they have a first-mortgage balance of $180,000. From a life-cycle perspective this family can gain substantially from borrowing now (since doing so will smooth their consumption in relation to their income). The credit card debt for this family currently stands at $20,000, on which they currently pay an annual interest rate of 19 percent. Although this family is prosperous and not financially distressed, the probability of finding it advantageous to file for bankruptcy and to use chapter 7 to extinguish credit card debt during the next five years is 20 percent.

If this family could pledge its future income without limit toward the settlement of its debt (a possibility excluded by current bankruptcy law), it could borrow $30,000 at an annual interest cost of 13 percent, and it would choose to do so. If this family converted its credit card debt into HLTV debt, it would be able to reduce bankruptcy risk and thereby save significantly on interest cost. Furthermore, the family would economize on taxes by converting credit card debt into mortgage debt (up to 100 percent of the value of the home). In the process of converting credit card debt to HLTV debt, the family might benefit by reloading—that is, expanding its total debt (to smooth consumption now that debt service costs are lower) and keeping some of that debt in the form of credit card payables.

To see why it can be desirable to reload, consider two possible scenarios for HLTV debt conversion: total conversion and partial conversion. Under total conversion the borrower chooses to borrow $30,000 from the HLTV lender. Under partial conversion the borrower chooses to borrow $20,000 from the HLTV lender and soon thereafter borrows an additional $10,000 from the credit card issuer. (This example of partial conversion probably overstates the extent of reloading. According to a recent survey, some 70 percent of HLTV borrowers reload. A typical example would combine an HLTV loan of $30,000 with a new credit card balance of $5,000 [Harney 1998].)

First, under either scenario the borrower is in a less vulnerable position (from the standpoint of after-tax interest cost) than before the HLTV loan. Assume that the family faces a combined (federal, state, and local) marginal tax rate of 50 percent, a credit card interest rate of 19 percent, and an all-in pretax cost of 14.7 percent on its HLTV loan (13.5-percent interest plus seven points with an expected maturity of six years). Before the HLTV loan the family's annual after-tax interest cost was $3,800 (19 percent of $20,000). Under the total-conversion scenario, the after-tax all-in cost of borrowing $30,000 is $2,950 (7.4 percent of $20,000 plus 14.7 percent of $10,000). Under the partial-conversion scenario, the after-tax all-in cost of borrowing $30,000 is $3,380. Clearly, under either scenario, the family can borrow much more at a lower total cost than before.

Why might the borrowers prefer the higher-cost partial-conversion scenario (which entails reloading)? If it wants to borrow the additional $10,000 for a short time, that option may be cheaper. In this scenario we assumed that the borrowing period was six years. But if the borrower needs the additional $10,000 only for two years, credit card borrowing will be cheaper, given the seven points charged on HLTV debt (which, as we have pointed out, is the lender's means of making prepayment risk more manageable in HLTV securitizations). Unsurprisingly some reloading occurs for the majority of HLTV borrowers.

Should Banks Be Discouraged from Making HLTV Loans?

The data reported about the high quality of HLTV loan portfolios and this discussion of the safeguards against churning and reloading imply that the movement of commercial banks into HLTV lending per se does not pose a threat to the stability of banks or to the deposit insurance fund. Indeed, as commercial banks move from credit card lending to HLTV lending, their portfolio risk should actually decrease (and the implicit value of deposit insurance protection that they receive should also fall) and *hold constant the FICO ratings of the loan customers served*. Nothing credible supports the claim that the spread of HLTV lending within the banking system will increase consumer default risk or destabilize the economy. Indeed, every consideration supports the opposite view. As HLTV lending replaces unsecured consumer lending, consumer default risk (and the risks borne by financial intermediaries) should fall, the cost of consumer credit should decline and become more stable, and the variance of consumption demand (a source of macroeconomic volatility) should be reduced.

Despite our confidence in the benefits of HLTV lending, it must be noted that the past year has seen substantial losses for several HLTV lenders, including Cityscape, Greentree, Preferred Mortgage, and Mego. The problems experienced by these firms typically reflected unrealistically optimistic assumptions about prepayment risk (combined with a declining interest rate environment), poor underwriting standards, and poor (or illegal) managerial practices. In the latter category, Mego (which is viewed by some as a victim of churning by its brokers) suffered in part because of its practice of rewarding brokers according to the number of originations produced (which encouraged them to entice borrowers to churn). Mego's problems illustrate a potential advantage of in-house origination—the avoidance of conflicting interests between originators and brokers—or at least the need to structure brokers' compensation carefully to be more incentive compatible.

These failures have underscored the wisdom of the more conservative approach to estimating risk taken by other lenders before 1998. Rating agencies, holders of securitized debt, and originators have learned from these experiences: what was viewed as conservative in 1996 is viewed as the industry standard in 1998. Like all financial innovations, HLTV lending will suffer some setbacks during its first years in existence as market participants learn how best to measure and to manage risk. (For details on the problems experienced by the various HLTV intermediaries in 1997–1998, see Timmons [1997b, d, e, j; 1998a, c]. See also La Monica [1997].)

6

HLTV Lending, Personal Bankruptcy, and Cram-Down

The concerns over reloading and churning described in chapter 5 have led some to attribute a significant role to HLTV lending in the rising personal bankruptcy trend over the past several decades. That is not a plausible view, both because reloading and churning are unlikely to be widespread (as argued above) and because HLTV lending is too small and too recent a phenomenon to have contributed significantly to aggregate bankruptcy trends.

Despite the growth in HLTV lending in recent years, other sources of consumer credit still dwarf it. As of the end of 1997, the HLTV lending industry made up only about 1 percent of the total mortgage industry and about 2.5 percent of the credit card industry. Furthermore, 125 percent HLTV lending has been a viable product only for the past five years. Increased consumer defaults have propelled the growth of HLTV lending, not vice versa (figure 6–1). Claims that HLTV lending causes bankruptcy to rise reflect a confusion between cause and effect.

Furthermore, analysts of recent trends in bankruptcy filings point to demographic changes as the primary force driving the new wave of consumer bankruptcies. Rising divorce rates, changing household patterns, increases in medical costs borne by individuals, and other factors (see figures 6–2 to 6–5) overshadow increases in consumer and mortgage debt or shoddy underwriting as

FIGURE 6–1
Personal Bankruptcies and HLTV Loan Growth,
1970–1996

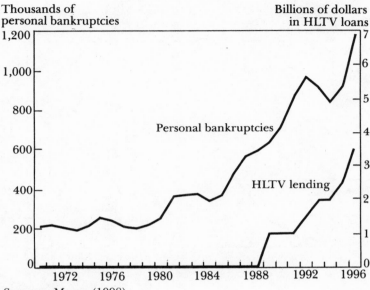

Source: Mason (1998).

the primary causes of the increase in personal bankruptcies over the past two decades (Mason 1998).

Misplaced concerns about the riskiness of HLTV
lending and the destabilizing effects of reloading and
churning have led some in Congress to advocate altering
personal bankruptcy law to allow cram-down—or bifur-
cation—of mortgage debt exceeding 100 percent of
home value. Under such a scenario a borrower filing
under Chapter 13 would avoid foreclosure. Mortgage
lenders would retain senior claims on the borrower up
to the amount of the fair market value of the underlying
property at the time of bankruptcy. The HLTV loan
would thus be second in line as a claim on borrower
wealth up to a maximum of the value of the mortgaged
property. The amount of the HLTV loan greater than
the value of the underlying property at the time of bank-

FIGURE 6–2
NUMBER OF PERSONAL BANKRUPTCIES AND NUMBER OF
HOUSEHOLDS WITH HEADS LESS THAN THIRTY-FIVE
YEARS OF AGE, 1960–1996

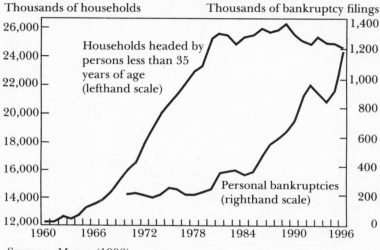

SOURCE: Mason (1998).

ruptcy would be treated as unsecured debt and placed on an equal footing in the bankruptcy process with other unsecured debt.

Such a fundamental change in the nature of the HLTV debt contract would undoubtedly undermine the special advantages of HLTV loans. By limiting the resources that stand behind the loan to the value of the mortgaged property itself, the law would transform HLTV lending from its current form—a relatively senior, collateralized claim on the consumer's wealth—to essentially a junior claim on the amount of housing wealth (but not the actual house) of the consumer. HLTV lending relies crucially on borrowers' perception that they might not be able to retain their homes if they were to declare bankruptcy and on the ability of the HLTV lender to use the threat of foreclosure or the inconvenience of a lien to lay claim to the consumer's nonhous-

FIGURE 6–3
CHANGE IN DIVORCE RATES BY AGE, 1970–1990

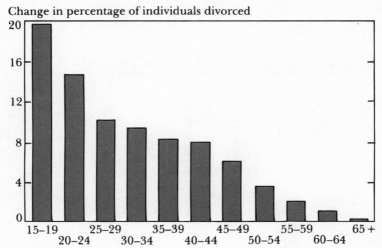

NOTE: Age is the age of the individual at the time of the divorce decree.
SOURCE: Mason (1998).

FIGURE 6–4
CHANGE IN PERCENTAGE OF INDIVIDUALS LACKING HEALTH INSURANCE BY AGE, 1987–1995

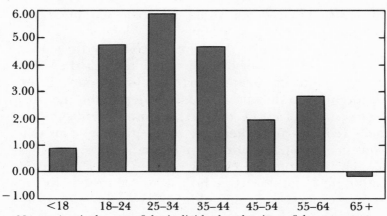

NOTE: Age is the age of the individual at the time of the survey.
SOURCE: Mason (1998).

FIGURE 6–5
Change in Incidence of Automobile Accidents, by Age of Drivers, 1970–1996

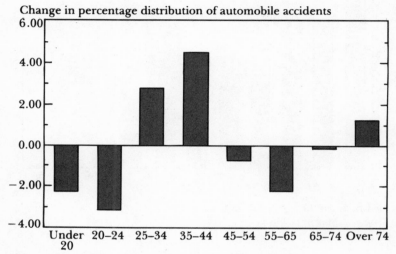

Change in percentage distribution of automobile accidents

NOTE: Age of the driver is at the time of the accident.
SOURCE: Mason (1998).

ing assets. Cram-down would essentially eliminate that special bargaining power of the HLTV lender.

Cram-down makes default more costly for the lender and less costly for the borrower. But ultimately the losers from cram-down are the borrowers. By removing the disincentive to default, and thus undermining the protected status of HLTV debt, cram-down would substantially reduce—and potentially eliminate—the gains that consumers reap from this form of lending.

There is concrete evidence of the adverse effects of imposing cram-down on borrowing contracts. In response to increasing agricultural distress in 1978, Congress instituted a temporary provision for mortgage cram-downs for family farmers under Chapter 12 of the Bankruptcy Act. The Chapter 12 provision was granted to alleviate hardships when farm values deteriorated so much that mortgage LTVs dropped below many farmers' outstanding mortgage balances. For the mortgage lenders the act was supposed to "provide restoration of the balance of fairness that [had] eroded in the bankruptcy courts in recent years as farmers remained liable for the excess LTV in bankruptcy" (Cumberland and Griffith 1979, 34).

As the farm debt crisis wore on, the Chapter 12 cramdown provision was extended in 1983, though not without recognition of its demonstrated economic shortcomings. "In March, the full House passed H.R. 416, which extends the law for another five years, until October 1, 1988. [The American Bankers Association] has resisted a simple extension, arguing that the chapter is lopsided and should be amended to give creditors a better deal, " as reported in "In Pursuit of a Balanced Bankruptcy Law," *ABA Banking Journal,* May 1983.

In 1986 the Bankruptcy Act was further amended, and by 1987 there was broad realization that the Chapter 12 provision had already induced a substantial adverse change in the supply of credit.

> The position of farmers in distress is radically changed by the . . . Chapter 12 farm bankruptcy statute coupled with the case of In re La Fond. . . . Under the La Fond case [even] large items of equipment that are necessary for the farm's operation are protected from creditors by the bankruptcy procedures. Because of these developments successful small farmers will have a more difficult time attracting financing and investment capital. (Willingham 1987, 74)

Bankers confirm that Chapter 12 cram-down has indeed made lending to small farmers a substantially riskier proposition, and they consequently have largely withdrawn funds from this business line.

> The present form of Chapter 12 has made it more difficult for marginal farmers and beginning farmers to obtain credit. Lenders tend to consider a worst-case scenario when analyzing credit requests, especially if the request is from a low-equity borrower and/or a younger, inexperienced one, and the worst case for a farm loan would be a Chapter 12 filing. The specter of a lender's hands being tied for years makes it more difficult to approve the loan request. Our bank has—and I'm sure other banks have—denied credit requests based partly on the chances of that scenario unfolding. (Burns 1992, 51)

The withdrawal of agricultural lenders took place when family farms sorely needed capital from all sources. But capital was not forthcoming from the banking sector. Figure 6–6 illustrates a profound change in farm

FIGURE 6–6
TOTAL FARM ASSET COMPOSITION, 1975–1997

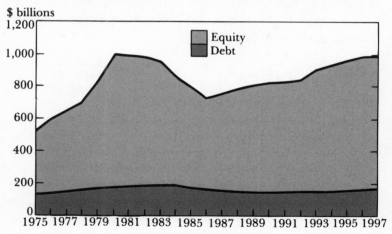

SOURCE: U.S. Department of Agriculture (1977).

debt-to-equity ratios during the 1980s. "Since bottoming at $137.9 billion in 1989, farm sector debt has expanded at an average annual rate of 1.6 percent to reach a level of $150.8 billion in 1995." Although farm debt was expected to reach $158 billion at year-end 1997, it "will still be nearly $36 billion less than the peak level of $193.8 billion owed at year-end 1984" (U.S. Department of Agriculture 1997, 1). Furthermore, although "nine years of increases in the value of [farm] land and buildings have restored $174 billion, or 72 percent, of the $243 billion in reduced values incurred between 1982 and 1986, [only] about $17 billion, or 31 percent of the sector's $55.9 billion reduction in debt that occurred between 1984 and 1989 has reappeared" (ibid., 2). As a result farm debt-to-equity ratios are lower than in the 1970s, before the 1980s farm crisis (figure 6–6).

That credit rationing forever changed the composition of the farming industry. The 1992 Census of Agriculture reported the fewest farms in existence since 1850. Furthermore, the industry was becoming more concentrated—17 percent of all farms in 1992 produced 83 percent of total sales (U.S. Department of Agriculture 1994). Although banks are now the source of some 65 percent of farm debt, table 6–1 shows that this is the debt of only the largest enterprises. Thus the composition of debt is quite different since the crisis.

Chapter 12 cram-down was supposed to be a special temporary measure to help family farmers during the crisis of the late 1980s. Instead, it has been officially extended twice by Congress and is expected to be made permanent under the National Bankruptcy Review Commission's proposals and resulting legislation (Cocheo 1997, 36). Although many agricultural specialists and others realize that such credit rationing has significantly reduced the viability of medium-sized farms, the practice unfortunately continues.

Cram-down radically affects credit allocation and

TABLE 6–1
FARM DEBT-TO-ASSET RATIOS, BY FARM SIZE, 1974–1989

	>$500,000	$250,000–500,000	$100,000–249,999	$40,000–99,999	$20,000–39,999	$10,000–19,999	<$10,000
1974	10.2	11.1	13.1	20.6	18.6	17.5	18.0
1975	9.7	10.9	12.8	20.3	18.2	17.4	18.0
1976	9.7	10.7	12.9	20.2	17.6	17.0	17.8
1977	10.1	11.3	13.5	21.1	18.3	17.8	19.0
1978	10.0	11.7	14.2	21.4	17.4	17.3	18.3
1979	10.6	12.5	15.2	21.6	17.4	17.4	18.2
1980	11.1	13.2	15.9	21.8	17.3	17.3	18.3
1981	12.4	14.9	18.1	24.1	18.8	18.7	19.9
1982	13.5	14.2	21.6	25.5	19.4	19.3	20.5
1983	12.9	14.5	22.2	25.3	20.1	18.9	20.2
1984	22.7	20.9	23.8	23.6	21.3	22.3	21.9
1985	23.3	21.1	24.1	24.1	21.6	22.2	22.4
1986	21.1	20.8	22.0	22.6	20.2	20.2	22.5
1987	31.4	22.7	20.3	18.4	14.3	10.4	14.8
1988	23.2	20.8	18.9	18.1	13.0	11.3	13.7
1989	19.9	17.9	18.7	15.6	12.7	12.3	16.3

NOTE: Series was discontinued after 1989.
SOURCE: Erickson et al. (1991).

does not support orderly and efficient allocation of resources in bankruptcy. In recognition of those facts, some current congressional proposals favor *restricting* cram-down extensions to consumer automobile lending and other areas under Chapter 13 (Seiberg 1998, 2). Cram-downs significantly hurt mortgage lending in agriculture in the 1980s. Cram-downs for home mortgage debt would result in the same type of credit contraction witnessed in the agricultural sector.

7
Conclusions

High loan-to-value lending is a fast-growing sector of the mortgage industry that has evolved to meet the needs of today's consumers and to compensate for the deficiencies of consumer bankruptcy law. HLTV lending allows consumers to commit credibly and voluntarily to not defaulting on consumer debt, and thus to use their home equity to reduce their debt service costs and to insulate consumption from temporary fluctuations in income.

Because the industry has expanded quickly—and competition has become fierce—some underwriting standards have been questioned. But lenders realize that the securitization that provides their funding base opens the industry to constant and detailed market scrutiny and discipline, and they have responded to that discipline by maintaining conservative lending standards, including high minimum credit scores and tight underwriting and monitoring guidelines.

HLTV lending is not the same as subprime lending. HLTV lenders serve clientele similar to those served by the better credit card issuers. HLTV lending is less risky than typical consumer loans extended through unsecured credit cards issued to the most creditworthy individuals (Coulton 1998).

The funding sources relied upon for HLTV lending add to its attraction. The expansion of securitization as a funding source for consumer credit effectively deepens U.S. debt markets in a fashion that can reduce the effects of economic recessions and speed recovery.

For all these reasons, HLTV lending is good for the American consumer and for the U.S. economy. If Congress singles this product out for expanding cram-down in personal bankruptcy, many consumers will lose access to an important source of low-cost lending.

References

Bary, Andrew. 1997. "In This Jittery Market, Could Asian Fears Be Overdone?" *Barrons*, December 15, pp. MW3–5.

Brockman, Joshua. 1998. "Secondary Market Seen Beckoning Small Banks." *American Banker*, February 3, p. 9.

Burns, Phillip. 1992. "Let Chapter 12 Sunset on Schedule." *ABA Banking Journal*, December, pp. 49–51.

Bush, Vanessa. 1997. "What Are B and C Loans?" *America's Community Banker*, November, p. 34.

Calomiris, Charles W. 1995. "Financial Fragility: Issues and Policy Implications." *Journal of Financial Services Research* 9: 241–57.

Calomiris, Charles W., and Mark S. Carey. 1994. "Loan Market Competition between Foreign and Domestic Banks: Some Facts about Loans and Borrowers." In *Proceedings of the Thirtieth Annual Conference on Bank Structure and Competition*, pp. 331–51. Chicago: Federal Reserve Bank of Chicago.

Caplin, Andrew, Charles Freeman, and Joseph Tracey. 1997. "Collateral Damage: Refinancing Constraints and Regional Recessions." *Journal of Money, Credit, and Banking*, pt. 1, November, pp. 496–516.

Clark, Kim. 1998. "125 Percent Mortgages: Asking for Trouble?" *Fortune*, March 30, p. 38.

Cocheo, Steve. 1997. "In Debt and Loving It." *ABA Banking Journal*, August, pp. 30–36.

Coulton, Antoinette. 1998. "VISA Launches No-Limit Card for People Making $100K." *American Banker*, April 1, p. 16.

Courter, Eileen. 1998. "Risky Business." *Credit Union Management*, February, pp. 26–29.

Cumberland, William E., and Christopher G. Griffith. 1979. "Bankruptcy Reform Act Restores Protection to Real Estate Secured Lenders." *Mortgage Banker*, January, p. 34.

DeYoung, Robert, and Daniel E. Nolle. 1995. "Foreign-Owned Banks in the U.S.: Earning Market Share or Buying It?" Economic and Policy Analysis Working Paper 95–2. Washington, D.C.: Office of the Comptroller of the Currency, April.

Erickson, Kenneth, Janusz Kubica, Duane Hacklander, Charles Barnard, James Ryan, and Helen Devlin. 1991. *Farm Sector Balance Sheet, including Operator Households, 1960–89, and excluding Operator Households, 1974–89, by Sales Class.* Statistical Bulletin 831. Washington, D.C.: U.S. Department of Agriculture.

Faulkner & Gray. 1998. *Home Equity Lending Directory: A Statistical Guide to B&C and Second Mortgage Lending.* New York: Faulkner & Gray.

Federal Home Loan Mortgage Corporation. 1997. *Credit Scores: A Win/Win Approach for Homebuyers, Lenders, and Investors.* Washington, D.C.: Freddie Mac.

FirstPlus Financial Group, Inc. 1997. *Annual Report.* SEC 10-K.

Fitch IBCA. 1998a. *FirstPlus Home Loan Owner Trust Series 1997–4.* New York: Fitch IBCA, January 29.

———. 1998b. *Securitization of 125 LTV Mortgages.* New York: Fitch IBCA, March 4.

Fitch Investors Service. 1996a. *ABCs of Credit Card ABS.* New York: Fitch Investors Service, LP, April 1.

———. 1996b. *A New Look at Subprime Mortgages.* New York: Fitch Investors Service, LP, December 16.

———. 1997. *Rating Subprime Home Equity Lenders.* New York: Fitch Investors Service, LP, March 3.

Flanagan, Chris, Ralph DiSerio, and Ryan Asato. 1998. "More Growth Ahead." *Mortgage Banking*, January, pp. 46–56.

Froass, Becky. 1997. "A Definition of Terms." *Mortgage Banking*, June, pp. 99–100.

Genesove, David, and Christopher J. Mayer. 1997. "Equity and Time to Sale in the Real Estate Market." *American Economic Review* (June): 255–69.

Glass, Rick T. 1997. "A Boom in B&C Retail." *Mortgage Banking*, March, pp. 65–72.

Goldberg, Lawrence G. 1992. "The Competitive Impact of Foreign Commercial Banks in the United States." In *The Changing Market in Financial Services*, edited by R. Alton Gilbert. Boston: Kluwer Academic Publishers.

Goldberg, Lawrence G., and Anthony Saunders. 1981. "The Determinants of Foreign Banking Activity in the United States." *Journal of Banking and Finance*, March, pp. 17–33.

Harney, Kenneth R. 1998. "Consumers Shift More Debt to Home Loans, Study Finds." *Washington Post*, July 4, p. E7.

Hewitt, Janet Reilley. 1997. "The Yuppie Loan." *Mortgage Banking*, October, pp. 177–78.

Kendall, Leon T. 1996. "Securitization: A New Era in American Finance." In *A Primer on Securitization*, edited by Leon T. Kendall and Michael J. Fishman. Cambridge: MIT Press.

Kochen, Neil. 1996. "Securitization from the Investor View." In *A Primer on Securitization*, edited by Leon T. Kendall and Michael J. Fishman. Cambridge: MIT Press.

Korell, Mark L. 1996. "The Workings of Private Mortgage Bankers and Securitization Conduits." In *A Primer on Securitization*, edited by Leon T. Kendall and Michael J. Fishman. Cambridge: MIT Press.

La Monica, Paul R. 1997. "In Brief: Cityscape May Lose Listing on Nasdaq." *American Banker*, December 19, p. 20.

Mason, Joseph R. 1998. "Demographic Influences and Personal Bankruptcies." Economic & Policy Analysis Working Paper. Washington, D.C.: Office of the Comptroller of the Currency.

Muolo, Paul. 1997. "High-LTV: High Octane for Profits." *US Banker*, December, pp. 73–76.

Nolle, Daniel E. 1995. "Foreign Bank Operations in the United States: Cause for Concern?" In *International Finance in the New World Order*, edited by H. Peter Gray and Sandra C. Richard. Oxford: Elsevier Science.

Prakash, Snigdha. 1997. "Feeling Better Now about High-LTV Loans? Don't, These Experts Say." *American Banker*, July 15, p. 16.

Roche, Ellen P. 1998. "Universal Accounts Could Make Mortgages Obsolete." *1997 Mortgage Market Trends*. Washington, D.C.: Freddie Mac, pp. 23–28.

Seiberg, Jaret. 1998. "Senate Panel Approves Bankruptcy Reform Bill." *American Banker*, April 3, pp. 1–2.

Talley, Karen. 1997. "Mainstream Mortgage Lenders Rebuff Wall St.'s High-LTV Push." *American Banker*, September 23, p. 1.

———. 1998. "Wall Street Watch: Small Banks Stepping Up High-LTV Securitizations." *American Banker*, January 20, p. 7.

Timmons, Heather. 1996. "Debt Fuels Boom in Equity Loans for More than Homes Are Worth." *American Banker*, December 17, p. 11.

———. 1997a. "Amid Bronx Cheers, High LTV Lenders Strut Their Stuff." *American Banker*, April 7.

———. 1997b. "Cityscape May Be Facing More Severe Problems As Stock Continues Slide." *American Banker*, October 28, p. 12.

———. 1997c. "Dallas Home Equity Lender Continues Its Buying Spree with a California Deal." *American Banker*, March 7, p. 7.

———. 1997d. "Greentree, Cityscape Take Big Hits, Rocking Specialty Finance Business." *American Banker*, November 17, p. 1.

———. 1997e. "Lower Restated Earnings Reveal Trouble in Subprimes." *American Banker*, November 21, p. 9.

———. 1997f. "Mego, Besieged High-LTV Lender, Insists It's Financially O.K., Denies Sale Rumors." *American Banker*, December 26, p. 20.

―――. 1997g. "New Portable Equity Loans Said to Cut Bug-Out Risk." *American Banker*, September 5, p. 6.

―――. 1997h. "PaineWebber Touts High-LTV-Backed Securities." *American Banker*, October 29, p. 8.

―――. 1997i. "Pioneer of High LTVs Is Still the One to Watch." *American Banker*, November 19, p. 12.

―――. 1997j. "Prepayment Woes Persist: Mego to Take a Big Charge." *American Banker*, December 10, p. 10.

―――. 1997k. "Proponents and Skeptics Debate High LTVs at Chicago Conference." *American Banker*, October 31, p. 10.

―――. 1998a. "Cityscape Selling U.K. Business to Ocwen for $477M." *American Banker*, April 2, p. 15.

―――. 1998b. "Ending Gain-on-Sale Would Hit Subprime Profits Hard, Say Oppenheimer, Fox-Pitt." *American Banker*, March 27, p. 8.

―――. 1998c. "From Depths of Subprime Pit, Mortgage Lenders Are Looking Up." *American Banker*, March 26, p. 1.

―――. 1998d. "High-LTV Battle Seen Brewing in Congress." *American Banker*, February 25, p. 9.

U.S. Department of Agriculture, Agriculture and Financial Statistics Division. 1994. *Fewest Farms since before the Civil War*. Washington, D.C.: Government Printing Office.

―――, Economic Research Service, Farm Structure and Performance Branch. 1997. *An Overview of the Current Farm Financial Situation and Outlook*. Washington, D.C.: Government Printing Office.

Wahl, Matthew, and Craig Focardi. 1997. "The Stampede to Subprime." *Mortgage Banking*, October, pp. 26–39.

White, Brenda, and Jack Levanthal. 1997. "The Allure of Mortgage Empires." *Mortgage Banking*, October, pp. 40–52.

White, Michelle J. Forthcoming. "Why It Pays to File for Bankruptcy: A Critical Look at Incentives under U.S. Bankruptcy Laws and a Proposal for Change." *University of Chicago Law Review*.

Willingham, Clark S. 1987. "Farm Bankruptcy Developments Cloud Agricultural Investment Opportunities." *Journal of Taxation of Investments,* autumn: 74–75.

Willis-Boyland, Anita. 1997. "Riding Herd on Subprime." *Mortgage Banking*, May, pp. 26–32.

Wilson, Caroline. 1997. "Home Equity Lending." *America's Community Banker*, July, pp. 22–27.

About the Authors

CHARLES W. CALOMIRIS is the Paul M. Montrone Professor of Finance and Economics at the Columbia University Graduate School of Business and an AEI visiting scholar. He is the director of the Program on Financial Institutions at the Columbia Business School and a research associate of the National Bureau of Economic Research.

Mr. Calomiris has written extensively about financial institutions, financial economics, and financial history. He is the recipient of a number of grants and awards in his field.

He is or has been a consultant on financial regulation for the Federal Reserve Board; the Federal Reserve Banks of New York, Chicago, and St. Louis; the World Bank; the Central Bank of Argentina; and the governments of Mexico, El Salvador, and China.

JOSEPH R. MASON is an assistant professor of finance at Drexel University College of Business and Administration. He specializes in financial and monetary economics, financial markets and institutions, and financial history. Current research focuses on measuring the macro- and microeconomic risks of financial intermediation.

DATE DUE

			PRINTED IN U.S.A.
GAYLORD			